MAJOR LEAGUE SPORTS

NHL

A Crabtree Branches Book

B. Keith Davidson

CRABTREE
Publishing Company
www.crabtreebooks.com

School-to-Home Support for Caregivers and Teachers

This high-interest book is designed to motivate striving students with engaging topics while building fluency, vocabulary, and an interest in reading. Here are a few questions and activities to help the reader build upon his or her comprehension skills.

Before Reading:
- What do I think this book is about?
- What do I know about this topic?
- What do I want to learn about this topic?
- Why am I reading this book?

During Reading:
- I wonder why...
- I'm curious to know...
- How is this like something I already know?
- What have I learned so far?

After Reading:
- What was the author trying to teach me?
- What are some details?
- How did the photographs and captions help me understand more?
- Read the book again and look for the vocabulary words.
- What questions do I still have?

Extension Activities:
- What was your favorite part of the book? Write a paragraph on it.
- Draw a picture of your favorite thing you learned from the book.

TABLE OF CONTENTS

The Game 4
Lighting the Lamp 6
Blazing Speed 8
On the Pond 10
The Art of the Body Check 12
Dropping the Gloves 14
What Makes a Beauty? 16
Stripes 18
Solid Between the Pipes 20
The Cup 22
The Great One 24
Sid the Kid 25
Connor McDavid 26
Carey Price 27
The NHL 28
Glossary 30
Index/Cool Facts 31
Websites for More Cool Facts 31
About the Author 32

THE GAME

Hockey is a game played with rubber on ice, two very unpredictable materials. The main idea behind the game is simple; put the puck in the net. The task is not that easy. Players need to be aware of the puck, of themselves, and of all the other players on the ice.

FUN FACT

Hockey is a combination of European stick and ball games such as hurley and shinny with Native American games such as lacrosse and tooadijik.

Montreal was home to the first indoor hockey game, on March 3, 1875.

The Buffalo Sabres and Minnesota Wild warm up on the ice before a game.

5

LIGHTING THE LAMP

Nothing makes a player happier than seeing the red goal light go on. It means that their team has scored.

Sidney Crosby

Wayne Gretzky

No one lit that lamp more than Wayne Gretzky with 894 career goals. There have been many famous goals over the years, such as the Golden Goal, scored by Sidney Crosby. It secured a gold medal for Canada at the 2002 Olympics.

FUN FACT

Mr. Game Seven, Justin Williams, earned that title scoring 15 points in nine trips to the seventh and deciding game of a playoff series.

7

BLAZING SPEED

NHL players have reached speeds of 30 mph (48 km/h) while playing the game. That is fast for a human, but the puck is moving even faster than that, often reaching speeds of over 93 mph (150 km/h).

FUN FACT

Pucks are kept in a freezer because warm pucks frequently bounce off the ice.

ON THE POND

Pond hockey is really where the game started to take shape. There were no **zones**, no **red line**, and no referees. Bobby Orr credited pond hockey for his unique style of play, as does **takeaway** master Mark Stone.

Bobby Orr and forward Wayne Cashman

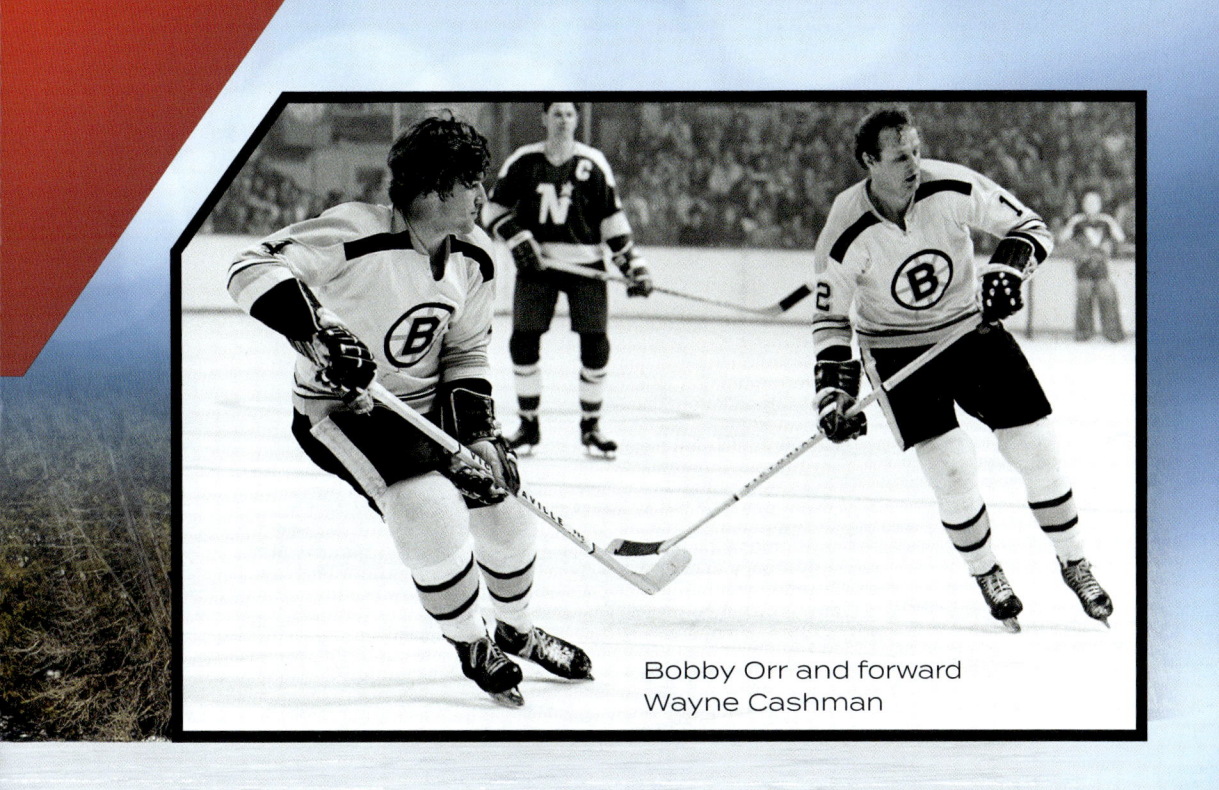

11

THE ART OF THE BODY CHECK

The body check is not simply flying across the ice to hurt someone. It involves finesse and skill. Whether it's a hip check, sending men spiralling to the ice, or a straightforward shoulder-to-shoulder hit, timing is everything.

Boston Bruins forward Chris Kelly checks New York Rangers forward Brandon Dubinsky and knocks him off his feet.

Bryce Slavador of the New Jersey Devils checks Boston Bruins forward Shawn Thornton.

FUN FACT

419 penalty minutes is the record in a game, and it happened when the Ottawa Senators met the Philadelphia Flyers March 5, 2004.

13

DROPPING THE GLOVES

For many fans, a fight is the most exciting moment in a hockey game. Two large men stand toe to toe and they trade blows until the linesmen break them up. It may seem **barbaric**, but there is a code of honor among the fighters. The goal is to send a message to the other team—not cause serious injury.

Dave Shultz holds the record for penalties in a season with 472 minutes.

15

WHAT MAKES A BEAUTY?

With a scar, or a few missing teeth, these faces may seem horrific to most people, but to a hockey player they are beautiful.

In hockey, "beauty" is a term used to describe an amazing teammate both on and off the ice. Playing through pain and at great risk of injury, a beauty is a hockey player who will do anything to win.

FUN FACT

Tie Domi had 333 fights in his NHL career, a record that stands to this day.

STRIPES

"C'mon, Stripes!" is something you're likely to hear at any hockey arena. The referees call **penalties** and decide what counts as a goal. The linesmen call **offsides** and **icing** the puck. A bad call can change the game completely. It's probably why fans get so mad.

The longest NHL game of all time happened in 1936—there were 116 minutes and 30 seconds of game time. The score at the end of the game's sixth overtime was 1-0 for the Detroit Red Wings. Long games are not a thing of the past though. On August 11, 2020, Brayden Point won a game for the Tampa Bay Lightning 2-1 in the fifth overtime period.

FUN FACT

On March 23, 1952, Bill Mosienko scored three goals in 21 seconds, giving him the record for fastest **hat trick** ever.

SOLID BETWEEN THE PIPES

No team can hope to make a run in the playoffs without finding a solid goaltender. Goalies like Carey Price, Jordan Binnington, and Marc-Andre Fleury have been known to carry teams.

Marc-Andre Fleury

Winning comes down to having more goals than the other team, and most of the time, that comes down to goaltending.

Carey Price

FUN FACT

Ben Scrivens made 59 saves on January 29, 2014— the most saves by a goaltender in a regular season shutout.

THE CUP

The NHL playoffs feature four rounds of gruelling seven-game contests. A team needs to win 4 games to move on. Teammates stick together through injuries and heartbreaking losses. If they manage to pull out a victory, their prize is the most famous trophy in all of sports, the **Stanley Cup**.

FUN FACT

Players get one day with the Stanley Cup all to themselves, and people have done some weird things with the trophy. It's been lost and thrown into rivers, but some people just want to eat cereal out of it.

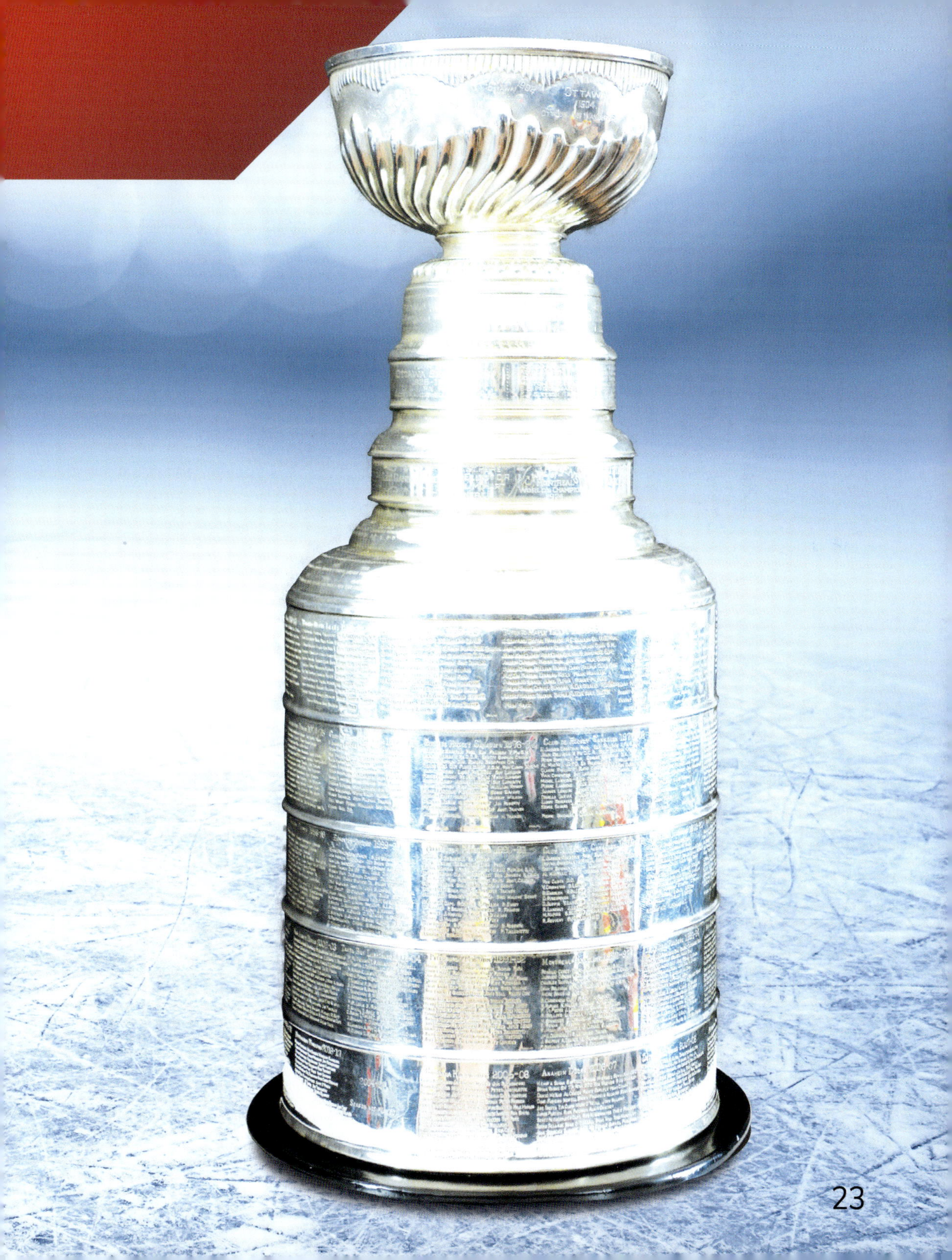

THE GREAT ONE
WAYNE GRETZKY

CAREER **1979-1999**

GAMES PLAYED	1,487
GOALS	894
ASSISTS	1,963
POINTS	2,857

AWARDS

10 Art Ross Trophies
5 Ted Lindsay Awards
1 Lester Patrick Trophy
9 Hart Trophies
2 Conn Smythe Trophies
5 Lady Byng Trophies
4 Stanley Cups

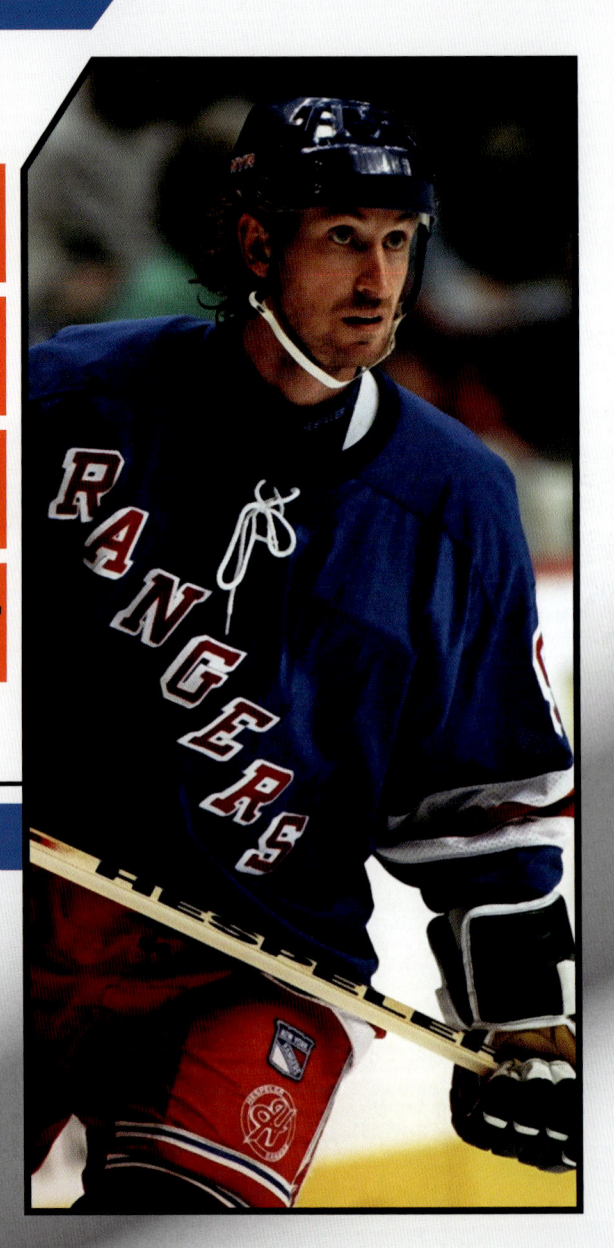

SID THE KID
SIDNEY CROSBY

CAREER 2005-PRESENT

GAMES PLAYED	984
GOALS	462
ASSISTS	801
POINTS	1,263

AWARDS

- 1 Mark Messier Leadership Award
- 2 Art Ross Trophies
- 2 Maurice Richard Trophies
- 3 Ted Lindsay Awards
- 2 Hart Trophies
- 2 Conn Smythe Trophies
- 3 Stanley Cups

CONNOR MCDAVID

CAREER 2015-PRESENT

GAMES PLAYED	351
GOALS	162
ASSISTS	307
POINTS	469

AWARDS

2 Art Ross Trophies
2 Ted Lindsay Awards
1 Hart Trophy

CAREY PRICE

CAREER **2007-PRESENT**

GAMES PLAYED	682
SAVE %	.917
GOALS AGAINST AVERAGE	2.49

AWARDS

1 Vezina Trophy
1 Ted Lindsay Award
1 Jennings Trophy
1 Hart Trophy

THE NHL

The dream of every young hockey player is to someday play in the NHL, to compete with the best players in the world, and play the game that they love.

FUN FACT

When a player scores a hat trick, or three goals, fans throw their hats on the ice. What happens to the hats? The player chooses one or two and the rest are held in case people want them back. After a week, the hats are donated to a charity.

Unofficially, a Gordie Howe hat trick is a goal, an assist, and a fight in one game.

29

GLOSSARY

barbaric (bar-BA-rik): Very cruel

hat trick (HAT TRIK): Three goals scored by the same player in a single game

icing (EYE-sing): The puck travels from before the center line past the other team's goal line without being touched

offside (OFF-side): A player enters the other team's zone without the puck

penalties (PEN-uhl-teez): Punishments in sports, usually decided by a referee

red line (RED LINE): The center line of the hockey rink

Stanley Cup (STAN-lee KUHP): The award for the best hockey team of the year

takeaway (TAYK-uh-way): Stealing the puck from another player

zones (ZOHNZ): Refers to a hockey rink's three zones: each team's zone and the middle neutral zone

INDEX

body check 12
fight(ers) 14
goals 7, 21, 28
Golden Goal 7
injury 14, 17
penalties 14, 18

playoff(s) 7, 20, 22
puck(s) 4, 8, 9, 18
referees 10, 18
Stanley Cup 22
zones 10

COOL FACTS:

Zdeno Chara holds the record for the fastest shot in the world, his slapshot has been clocked at 108.8 mph (175 Km/h).

In 1979, Ron Hextall became the first goalie to ever score a goal by shooting the puck into an open net.

Does bad blood run in families? Brothers Dale and Tim Hunter both have over 3000 penalty minutes making them numbers 2 and 8 on the all-time leaders' board.

WEBSITES FOR MORE COOL FACTS:

www.hockeycanada.ca/multimedia/kids

https://facts.kiddle.co/Ice_hockey

http://howtohockey.com

ABOUT THE AUTHOR
B. Keith Davidson

B. Keith Davidson grew up playing with his three brothers and a host of neighborhood children, learning about life through sports and physical activity. He now teaches these games to his three children.

We recognize that some words, team names, and designations, for example, mentioned herein are the property of the trademark holder. We use them for identification purposes only. This is not an official publication.

Crabtree Publishing Company

Produced by: Blue Door Education for Crabtree Publishing
Written by: B. Keith Davidson
Designed by: Jennifer Dydyk
Edited by: Tracy Nelson Maurer
Proofreader: Ellen Rodger

Cover: Top photo © Shutterstock.com/ Oleksii Sidorov, players © Kathy Willens/ Associated Press, PG 4: ©shutterstock.com/vkilikov, PG 5: ©istock.com/bigjohn36 (top), © Gale Verhague/ Dreamstime.com, PG 6: ©Alexander Mirt| Dreamstime.com, PG 7: Gretsky image © Håkan Dahlström https://creativecommons.org/licenses/by-sa/3.0/ Sidney Crosby © VancityAllie.com/ CCAT2.0 www.creativecommons.org/licenses/by/2.0/deed.en, PG 8: shutterstock.com/Eugene Onischenko, PG 9: shutterstock.com/Christopher Bailey, PG 10-11: LesPalenik / Shutterstock.com, PG 11: © Jerry Coli| Dreamstime.com (inset), PG 12: ©Jerry Coli| Dreamstime.com, PG 13: ©Jerry Coli| Dreamstime.com, PG 14: shutterstock.com/kovop58, PG 15: ©Fahrner| Dreamstime.com(top), ©Scott Anderson| Dreamstime.com, PG 16: © Albertshakirov| Dreamstime.com, PG 17: ©Jerry Coli| Dreamstime.com(top), ©Secondarywaltz/ CCA2.0www.creativecommons.org/licenses/by/2.0/deed.en, PG 19: Jai Agnish / Shutterstock.com, PG 20: ©Jerry Coli| Dreamstime.com, PG 21: ©Jerry Coli| Dreamstime.com (top), ©Jerry Coli| Dreamstime.com, PG 23: ©Meunierd| Dreamstime.com, PG 24: © Håkan Dahlström https://creativecommons.org/licenses/by-sa/3.0/ PG 25: ©Jerry Coli| Dreamstime.com, PG 26: ©Gints Ivuskans| Dreamstime.com, PG 27: ©Jerry Coli| Dreamstime.com, PG 28: ©Jerry Coli| Dreamstime.com, PG 29: ©shutterstock.com/Master1305.

Library and Archives Canada Cataloguing in Publication

Title: NHL / B. Keith Davidson.
Other titles: National Hockey League
Names: Davidson, B. Keith, 1982- author.
Description: Series statement: Major league sports | "A Crabtree branches book." | Includes index.
Identifiers: Canadiana (print) 20210220341 |
   Canadiana (ebook) 2021022035X |
   ISBN 9781427155221 (hardcover) |
   ISBN 9781427155283 (softcover) |
   ISBN 9781427155344 (HTML) |
   ISBN 9781427155405 (EPUB) |
   ISBN 9781427155467 (read-along ebook)
Subjects: LCSH: National Hockey League—Juvenile literature. |
   LCSH: Hockey—United States—Juvenile literature. |
   LCSH: Hockey—Canada—Juvenile literature.
Classification: LCC GV847.8.N3 D38 2022 | DDC j796.962/64—dc23

Library of Congress Cataloging-in-Publication Data

Names: Davidson, B. Keith, 1982- author.
Title: NHL / B. Keith Davidson.
Other titles: National Hockey League
Description: New York : Crabtree Publishing Company, 2022. |
   Series: Major league sports | "A Crabtree Branches Book."
Identifiers: LCCN 2021022545 (print) |
   LCCN 2021022546 (ebook) |
   ISBN 9781427155221 (hardcover) |
   ISBN 9781427155283 (paperback) |
   ISBN 9781427155344 (ebook) |
   ISBN 9781427155405 (epub) |
   ISBN 9781427155467
Subjects: LCSH: National Hockey League--History--Juvenile literature. |
   Hockey--United States--History--Juvenile literature. | Hockey--Canada--History--Juvenile literature.
Classification: LCC GV847.8.N3 D368 2022 (print) | LCC GV847.8.N3 (ebook) | DDC 796.962/6406--dc23
LC record available at https://lccn.loc.gov/2021022545
LC ebook record available at https://lccn.loc.gov/2021022546

Crabtree Publishing Company
www.crabtreebooks.com   1-800-387-7650

Printed in the U.S.A./072021/CG20210514

Copyright © 2022 **CRABTREE PUBLISHING COMPANY**

All rights reserved. No part of this publication may be reproduced, stored in a retrieval system or be transmitted in any form or by any means, electronic, mechanical, photocopying, recording, or otherwise, without the prior written permission of Crabtree Publishing Company. In Canada: We acknowledge the financial support of the Government of Canada through the Canada Book Fund for our publishing activities.

Published in the United States
Crabtree Publishing
347 Fifth Avenue, Suite 1402-145
New York, NY, 10016

Published in Canada
Crabtree Publishing
616 Welland Ave.
St. Catharines, ON, L2M 5V6